D1235698

Mysterious Acts by My People

Valerie Wetlaufer

Alexander, Arkansas
www.SiblingRivalryPress.com

Sibling Rivalry Press, LLC
13913 Magnolia Glen Drive
Alexander, AR 72002

www.siblingrivalrypress.com
info@siblingrivalrypress.com

ISBN: 978-1-937420-66-6

Library of Congress Control Number: 2013956735

First Sibling Rivalry Press Edition, March 2014

For

Elizabeth Huddleson

1982-2003

•

Ja**N**eill **W**eseloh

1984-2006

•

Laura **H**ershey

1962-2010

I. A Constant Frenzy to Disguise

II. Scent of Shatter

III. The Inability to Hold Particles Together

Mysterious Acts by My People

"Polish the sin until it shines."

— Alice Notley

I

A CONSTANT FRENZY TO DISGUISE

SOLITARY VICE

I loved a girl
when I was a girl,

before I knew desire
could be used against me.

I so wanted to be relevant.
Simple exchange—

bouquets of wheat.
My dirt-stained hands,

tangled hair. I never
could be prim,

in apple-pie order.
I dropped all the eggs,

licking their smear
off my hands;

wrinkled her ribbons
into my pocket,

tore pages from her books,
all for the sake

of the lonely hour.

BAD WIFE SPANKINGS

My wedding dress is stale in the closet.
You crumble drunk on the stairs,
still plagiarizing your vows,

while elsewhere, girls are getting married.
The tablecloth wilts beneath the roast
& the cats lap up the melting butter

before it hardens in the china dish.
The buried box, full of all your gifts—
regret, tattoos, razorblades, a limping pit bull.

I am the archeologist, digging through this city,
scrubbing your shit stains from the toilet,
unearthing the hidden town below us

where my dress was clean & you were happy.
I rewrite myself while you lie about dancing so close,
dreaming of me, & putting your whole hand inside her.

I saw her car in the parking lot.
I saw your lips on her neck
& her cock in your hand.

MYSTERIOUS ACTS BY MY PEOPLE

They say you can get two redheads
for the price of one in this town.
I myself have held most. Kinky
boots & cat suits; the votaries
of tight-lacing; trickledown perversion.

In this town we share a constant frenzy
to disguise. Pages turn. Footsteps rustle
the dust. Combs glide through hair.
Straighten your wig & oil my tattoos.
Ponder the liquification of clothes.

More of my bones were broken in hospitals
than the playground, a corrective violence
done to heal my deformities.

The shoe as weapon & wound.
I drag my unreliable leg on the left.
I am not in the mood for song.
The piano is covered in soot & I listen
as nails are filed, costumes mended.

TORNADO ALLEY

Last night I dreamt about my teeth again

        the borders of my body bruised

the bloodstains on the shoulders of all my shirts

        & all my bedding.

With my finger slowly I scrawl your name

                & if touch were bearable . . . or memory . . . or the voice of . . .

I stayed down when they pushed

        me down   I stayed on the bottom

The old couple threw fried chicken at us

        when we kissed   A proclamation to the world.

My tongue tasted salt, iron, the same

            taste as barbed wire used to bind

her hands

        A boy or a girl is only a boy or a girl
            until someone tells them otherwise.
        Endorsing these lifestyles to the young
            of tender ages confuses them and causes violence.

These were the longest years of our lives.

Carry a roll of quarters

Carry the rape flashlight, advertised to blind

　　your persecutor　　　　I stopped wearing anything but black

Tried

　　　　to die　　　　　　It would've been the 33rd

gay suicide that year　　　　　　　I let all my tattoos burn

Thanks be to God, who is mighty in battle.

Did something happen to your arm?

　　　Is that paint?　　　　　　Are you bleeding?

UNSENT

Trees are being kept busy with waving.
I tie bundles of letters I didn't have the heart
to send you, tie them with thin ribbon & hide
them high on a shelf. I sleep on my stomach
& wake up sore, like I've washed up on a beach
somewhere, my skin sunburnt, my elbows scarred.
I pray every day for the moon to erase your face
from my mind, but still light pools at the foot
of the bed & my mind has memorized
your phone number without me telling it to.
There are so many things I want to say, but I
fold them, envelope them, address them, hide them
up on that shelf, in the closet where we carved
our names on the door jamb. I wake up,
scuff my heels against the floor, go on being starved.

CONJUGAL ELEGY

Pillows & ribbons harness barefoot friends,
    haughty sisters & smiles; mothers watch, snoring.
  Dirty Jeep, broken January; darkness steals my grief.
     I cannot imagine something more fragile than marriage.
You held my hand.
    We listened to the Callas arias on our porch.
  You kept rewinding the love song back to the beginning
    to the place where she sings, *Certainly not today.*

  Leaf shadows tent walls. My tongue traces
    tattoos & scars. Strange shirts
 mingle in the dryer. Tangled sand, uncomfortable
    legs, wasted days spent memorizing the body
 I'd soon share. Bride, bridge, bridle; all signs said,
     Don't wife her.

I have learned how to hollow beginnings,
    rewind homes & wedding veils.
  Your drool, the doorknob, clumsy knots.
    Today the map is mortified.
In bed, polka dots, miscarriage.
    Weather changes leaves, fragile-making.
(not even divorcing, in the eyes of the law: *dissolving)*

I remember my sorrow at finding ants housed in my mother's peonies.
   When we moved, the new residents tore out all her flower beds,
the strawberry patch & the treehouse. I drove you there to show you.
     You held my hand.

GRAMMAR FOR EVERYONE

Canadians love European architecture & literature.

Even the dogs seem happy here.

I told Jacques no, but I said yes to Pierre.

You can't even imagine the things I say to myself.

I am aware of the error I have committed.

It is only polite to extinguish your cell phone in the theater.

Wise children will be rewarded.

The same three boys. Every five days.

I want one bottle. I want several bottles. I don't want a single bottle.

Paper is expensive. The sun shines all year over there.

Don't take that route, take the other, you will arrive much faster.

Jacques & Alice met some very ugly men & women.

A fat chicken will hardly suffice for his dinner.

Because of her, the big mahogany table is broken.

The table is broken.

Pierre is gone.

She always picks the least beautiful flowers.

Pierre thinks of his parents.

Jacques saw Pierre, but he did not greet him.

No matter what decision you make, I will leave.

My neighbor, a well-known journalist, explained the whole affair to me.

The wine is better in Europe than in the United States.

LOVE POEM IN THREE PARTS

1.

I knew you only by your clothes for the longest time:
a soft cotton shirt, worn thin, ribs whaleboned, framed.
One day you emerged in different vestments & I
walked on confused. Your skin burned my palm
when I dared touch you; your nipples pointed north.

2.

In Florida, it rains like God hates you. I walk alone
& bitten by harsh plashes. The coffee is watered
down. Everything diluted. Your voice, hollow
across the country, pinging along cables, digitized
& empty. You say, *Let lips do what hands do*, tracing
my nipples with your tongue, drawing the syllables
out, wrapping your voice around me as I giggle.
I want your fist inside me.

3.

You're so pretty. It's what my mother can't stop
saying. She's thinking about those glossy girls
in magazines I kissed until the pages were limp
& newsprint showed through the faces. You
are twisting dreaded locks between two fingers
& watching my father slowly sip his coffee.
He's trying not to regard your nipples. We
were caught in the rain. Your thin cotton shirt
is soggy & transparent. You've spelled love
on my neck. A bruise is a bruise. The phone
rings & rescues my parents with details
to attend. The party is tomorrow. We are wearing

white & clasping hands. We sleep like silverware
in my childhood bed. Through thin walls we hear
my parents talk & fuck. You dip your face
into me like a kitten drinking milk, your whole face
disappearing into the shallow bowl.

JULY

This is no season for harvest.
Nothing blooms.
Babies don't germinate in your womb.
I practice calisthenics.
You trim fat from the meat.

Your lips meet mine.
I tell you so.
I love your affection for Space.

In aged living rooms
pajamas jumped like bunnies,
children dressed in astronauts.
A documentary on the landing.
We watch, forty years ago, moon dust.

The canals are flooding
for ten seasons I hear.
I have not been to Paris.
Drops decorate the pond.
It rains. Slick grass sticks.

ANATOMY

Our fascination with nature & the natural form:
    fashion moved beyond feathers
        (your wedding brooch
            made from the talon of a falcon)
to other parts of bird anatomy & eventually
    the entire bird.

My best lines to you are composed on vellum, the skin of a stillborn lamb.
    I scrape the hide clean,
        remove the hairs & rub it smooth with pumice.
    Then washed, dressed with chalk & finished
      with a lime bath. This parchment is known
        for the absence of imperfection.

You press yourself tightly to me. Whalebone corsets keep us erect.
    Breath escapes. All I smell
      is hollow bones & flight.

THE CANYON

It rains in the forest. My feet dip into cool streams of water pock-marked by the storm. Soon the drops will slow. Creatures will emerge from the foliage. I shall hide here, in the pine dust, to wait, to watch. A moose masticates; an elk leaps. What will happen when I leave? Will the animals continue on without me? Will the rain? My footprints will wash away. The same with my memory. Only you stand clear in my mind, your yellow-flowered dress, the sun reflecting off the comb in your hair. The way our knees touched. How sweaty you tasted & sweet. One day I will no longer be strong enough to reach this place.

It is raining. My hair sticks to my face. Rivulets cut a path through the dirt on my ankles. This rock is unsteady, moss-covered, slick. Bushes rustle beside us. A creature appears; I do not know what name to call it. There is a chill in the air. The canyon breathes. I was not always as I seem. Once my hair grew long. You braided it together with your own. A black & blonde plait held us together on the ground. I put a pebble in your mouth. You almost kissed me.

The rain stains the path before me a dark gray, settling each mote of dust into submission. You make notes of each animal we encounter. You record the palmate antlers of the bull moose, that *elg* is Swedish for elk & the distinctive feathers of a Steller's Jay. I am a stranger in this land. I gaze at our knuckles, clasped. How tan your skin is next to mine. How rough & small your fingers. I have taken off my boots. I have slipped my feet into the stream. The water is glacial & clear. You ask me what name I want to be called. I cannot bear to return here alone.

REMARKS ON COLOR

1. There is no such thing as love
   but there are love problems.

        2. (How difficult to resist sucking
              the knuckles of the dental
     hygienist, her breasts so close, & she
           so generous with the nitrous.)

3. Green walks a dog. She does not
       know the dog is brown. She does not
   know I perceive her as beloved.

      4. (What is love?
           a) opaque,
           b) transparent
           c) greenish-brown)

5. What if the dog Green walks is not her own?

      6. The color of my mouth
           after brushing my teeth
     resembles the color of my mouth
         after kissing the dental hygienist.

7. The difficulties we encounter
       when we reflect on the nature
   of love are embedded in the indeterminateness
       of our concept of sameness of love.

      8. I feel love.
     I observe love. (Love does not stand
         for the same concept in the first
     & second sentences.)

9. Imagine my beloved Green &
       the dental hygienist meet
   one day; would they recognize they
       both belong to my lips?

      10. Let us hope not.

YOUR BODY WILL HAUNT MINE

Always worried
you'd lift your shirt
urge my hand to palpate
your breasts checking for lumps.

Your mother died at twenty
haunting you
threatening to appear
at any moment—
an unfamiliar bump
a freckle that wasn't before.

Your head aches.
I say it's nothing.
I scoff, kiss you.
My imagining
can cure all.

I am in France
when I get the call.
An infection
of the thin
lining of the brain.

You were twenty
& no longer mine
to mourn.

LATE RUSSIAN

When I loved a Kremlinologist,
she wrote me letters in Cyrillic
but refused to decipher them.

For months we planned a trip
to Moscow, but never left.
She shushed me to sleep with tales

of Marxism, Stalinism,
& Polish surnames.
When I loved an horologist,

I got a watch for my birthday three
years in a row; tiny cogs & hands
spun around. We argued over digital

versus analog, leather wristbands or cloth.
She was never late for an appointment,
but the ticking in our house drove me mad.

This is not a sweet story. We stood in a forest,
one woman on either side of me. We gazed
past each other, into the place where the trees

housed a clearing. They left together.
One had an accent, one small hands.
The snow retained our footprints.

Don't you dare be gentle with me.
Not with your strong forearms.

TWINS

Look at my babies. They twist in their crib,
they spit up & gurgle but they do not cry.

I have decorated the nursery with purple clouds & clowns,
though I think the circuses & storms frighten them.

Later I will bathe them in the sink, blowing in their faces
so their eyes will close when the water runs down.

I feared their birth &, in the end, my body wouldn't
let them go. The doctor split open my stomach & pried them.

Their legs were tangled together unnaturally; malformed.

They will wear braces & casts to straighten their limbs
& the stares from other mothers in the street: unbearable.

Only one of them will live. I have to choose.

ELK SONG

The sound as if a prehistoric bird were hunting.

Along the trail, we pause. The air has gotten thinner.

I am in search of a fashionable animal:

velvet-covered antlers, new coat for every season.

Forest shadows persist. We put one foot before the other,

climbing. Again this bugling. I collect stones to line up

by the window, to bring the mountain inside.

Forward from the brush steps a bull, crown of antlers four feet wide.

You do not know what to call it,

but I have the scrap of a name on my tongue.

CITY OF SALT—

my tongue is never sated.
Your sky is gray & inverted.
Here I clothe myself in white.
My breath appears before me
& you whisper my name
through the veil.
Like wax I am sealed.
Night—the air is cool.
Your presence announced,
the slope of land beneath
my feet propels me
toward adamellite.
You whirl through my
attempts at parentheses.
Large, young, my frame
consoles you before the tomb,
granite elegy, ruins warmed
by the sun, I recall estranged
details; your allergy for bees,
the aftertaste of sea air
on your breath; knowing
your sin. Beyond the
crumbling, the dog
bones, pizza crusts,
used syringes & dust.
The letters I tied
with ribbon to the trees.
Unable to conceive
of defeat, the asp
slithers into the hollow
beneath our bed.
Apparitions startle milk
from my chest
the terror you used against me.

I GAVE YOU MY—

carefully folded, swooned, postpartum

posthaste—

my letter to you, I gave—

curious, you said uncanny you

said the color of my eyes in this light

is a different shade of green said

you don't eat meat but you wear

leather outside the birds

& inside the sun on the chair

& my thighs spread &

stick to the plastic &

you said you loved

it & the ampersand & my swoon

silently inside my skirt & the ochre

on the building changes to umber

in the light & the tree outside is

bare & I am, my foot inside my slipper

my toes curled behind & ow & yes

& some days are sunny days & some

days are

UNLIKE YOUR SISTER

The door was locked when I arrived.
I had no choice but to force entry.

Head ragged, no crow halo as I'd imagined—
lucky I brought a wig for you to wear.

Better this way; you resemble your sister.
You need something new & I am new.

Faith demands no restrictions;
I trust you to lie still beneath me.

Your beautiful feet—nails spared a garish
red, you need no garnish for your beauty.

Unlike your sister.

Your body rises when you smell me
& you say my name, eager already,

voice pinched & hungry.
I kick the dog, slam the door.

You struggle in your excitement

& your teeth mark scalloped edges
into my arm as I hold you still.

When we met, I was fourteen
& you were nine. We played hide

& seek. I hid myself inside you
& was never found.

BEFORE THE DIAGNOSIS

We chase after autumn
which has not yet arrived
in our valley. You pack
a lunch. I fill the back seat
of our Jeep with woolen garments
knitted long ago, when we lived
among the Green Mountains
& never feared the fall.

We drive east into the canyon.
Up & up. You think you spot
one red leaf, but it is blight. Surely
somewhere yellow aspens conceal
elk at this elevation.

At last beyond the ski resorts
we settle on the trail & start walking.
Last year at this time, there was snow.

My fevers keep us awake most nights,
& though you chide, I insist
on plunging my feet into the stream.
You wash them, kiss each toe & warm them,
wrapped in your lap, in a scarf.

Alpine flowers still bloom. I pick one
for each of us to tuck into our braids.
Yours wraps around your forehead.
Mine hangs down my back, though
the hair is thinning at the roots. We are

afraid of the future. Small amounts
of red & yellow have existed

in the leaves all along, concealed
by green chlorophyll. The cold

brings on the color, but my forehead
is so warm. I want one leaf of every
shade to seal between wax & hang
by my bedside for when the weather turns.

THE FOURTH MISCARRIAGE

I would rather write

about a toddler

instead of dilation & curettage,

or the M word

so much harder to say,

as if you had done something wrong;

a misstep—ankle turned on the curb,

your gait broken by a fall.

How at first we joked about your body:

so good at getting pregnant,

so bad at staying pregnant.

Even now when I see the swell

of a gravid body, or hold the precarious

weight of a child against my chest, I flash

to the night I found you

digging through the clumps

of tissue in the toilet

bowl still bleeding on

the bathroom floor because

that was our son & you needed

to find him & we needed

something to bury.

II

SCENT OF SHATTER

PRAYER

Master, thou hast searched me & known me,

by the rivers of Dubuque.

The night was dark. You parted the reeds.

Whither can I hide the darkness from thee?

You are intimately acquainted with my ways.

Bless the little slaughters, lambs in the fields.

I waited by my window for thee last night.

The stars shone brightly through the pane, lovely diamonds.

I could not resist their scattering.

Bless this forsaken lass; my troubles not to be endured.

Surely thou wilt let me slay the wicked.

Depart from me therefore, ye bloody men.

In the name of the Holy Ghost,

I consecrate this valley of tears, this Wisconsin.

FULL IMMERSION

At the age of nine, Pa drove me
to the river. The pastor & deacons
awaited. I donned a white robe,
transparent, self-conscious
of my fresh nubs.

Father Jonas reached beneath me,
placed a hand over my nose & mouth.

I resisted.

He pushed me hard until my feet released
& rose to the surface, like a corpse.

I cried afterward, cold & clammy,
wet hair plaited back.

All the men thought I was full
of the Holy Ghost.

TELLING TRUE

Nineteen when he forced me—
marked his hand's print on my skin.
I tried to peel the purple bruises away;
so much stuck beneath my nails.
The red water wouldn't stop coming.

Pa married me to that man,
he who put the child inside.
Locked in cooking—spilled flour
& eggs. Marcus beat the baby still.
Bread wouldn't rise. I was made
to abandon my books & slates.

Not even Ma believed I told true.
I cut open the window to see outside.
All figured wrong—that I broke my own hair,
tore my dress & stained. I rattled on
& they put me away.

Scrawled notes through the cage to boys
who threw rats to share my bread.
White-clad men held me below ripples
til the screaming stopped.
Ropes held strong, but glass

abounds—mirror glass shows a picture of me.
A window: water, looking in. No one believes
I have done no wrong. They have stole
my shoes, but Brother sent a dress
for Fancy Mary to visit Town.

Doctor doses twice a day; water's clear here,
head abuzz & doubling. He lifts my slip
& gives my medicine. Says it stops the dreams,
but sleep just doesn't come. Savage noises
hunt the night. I make myself small & quiet.

FOUNDERING

There was no sound,
& then there was nothing but sound.
Folks say I stopped the baby myself.
Would that I knew how.

All day I stand at the kitchen window
of our house in Town, far from my parents' farm.
His mother bakes & calls me a Whore.
We are lucky to have one tree beside the porch.
Shade in the summer. I make tea in the sun & sleep,
sheets of leaf shadows over my body.
That's when my belly grows still. My hair
stops growing, then it grows too fast.
The colors change like autumn.
All the color drains.

The baby grows inside me still,
though my belly remains slack.
I hear its whisperings, its wants.
The tree scratches fingers on the ceiling.
Neighbors peek inside the windows;
voices, loud poundings on the door.
The preacher, the doctor, everyone
comes to call. But I'm too occupied
to entertain. There's never enough
milk or beef tea for the baby's satisfaction.
Men always want more.

As a child, I churned butter, mooed
with the cows. I wore my hair in braids.
Fresh straw for a bed was abundant.
No one in sight for miles but livestock.
Quiet like you've never heard.

Here I scratch my story in dirt on the walls;
eventually they sweep me away.

SELECTIONS FROM THE ASYLUM NURSES' REPORTS

Patient cites Horses heard beyond the walls, galloping.

Manages resistance to moral therapy.

*

Screaming will not stop!

*

Doctors say Vices have led to this madness.

Hydrotherapy shows no effect.

*

Patient shows strange affinity for locomotives, imagines she is roped down,
survives through faith.

Husband's visits have ceased since dementia
increases in intensity with his presence.

*

Patient observed dosing with cocaine (prescribed by Doc Griffel in Eau
Claire). Inhalations incite mania, but liquid solution brushed on pudenda,
as in similar cases, proves calming. Doctor Ludwig treats her twice daily.

*

Winters are brisk & snowfall common,
but the patient complains of heat sores.

*

Such a breeze through these halls, to the bone & hungry; whispers thick
& swift as warriors.

*

Mary Sweeney has escaped! We chart her progress by the newspaper:

So much smashing & destruction.
She spreads her fear about the land.

INSTRUCTION PIECE

Sometimes the sun comes along too strong.
In situations such as this, raccoons
            are the only solution. Their hands clean swift
& pick locks. They find their way through
            any hole. Nurse says my hair would make a fine nest.

I refuse to bury underwater. This makes a stench of my perfume
            that drives the guards away. They call me Missus,
but Mister never shows himself. I've changed the locks
            on my curls & eschewed a kitchen wife.

Baby gone, sickness or tainted blood, no matter.
            Husband also no more. I am a cat. I tuck my paws
beneath me & lick the fleas clean.
            Kind church women think I ought to read.
They lend me abridgements of their holy fire. Doctor
            refuses me medicine while I read so my wick
burns down all night as the pages move.

I live in the belly of a wail, swimming in the ocean
            Ma's family came across. I stand in a circle & pray—
flames tickle my ankles but I do not burn.

I lay small & wished for a grave, but still persist.
            Next door, the cell is shared by a prophetess.
She sees a river parting ways, escape & slavery unbound.

She tells of the spring her husband threw a blade
            & the shelves toppled. Redness followed as she swept each plate,
cup & bowl away into the garden. She whispers every dish cracking
            & I run my hands along my body, rivers falling
from my face. I have never heard music sweeter.

THE WINDOW-SMASHER SPEAKS

I am the one drawn to shards,
the pieces of things left behind
when something larger breaks.

For now, I am confined to my oubliette;
lack of food, lack of light—
alone with your Dominion.

You tell me frost dances on panes
already; I am eager to keep House
in the Snow.

The Rowan is in bloom.
Pestle the flowers & berries together
for a fleshy paste to ease one's captors.

Soon I will travel by train
through every town, bound
for the November house,
the space between two seasons.

GLASS MAKES A CLEAN CUT

I mark my own body with bruises,
trying to recreate your damage.

No amount of study will free me.

Glass makes a clean cut.

My name doesn't sound the same
without your mouth around it.

MUTINY

Townsfolk whisper all my puppies don't bark.

I enjoy the quiet.

The frost-smoke obscures sound & I alone must break the air.

I walked around the town all night, told a man I was a live dictionary.

The paper says I lost the job, escaped a widow, stole a switch, did my sums.

I do recall a desk, a dress, spectacles perchance.

Either way, there's a lesson.

I sip ale by the fire.

I don't know what kind of hair-pin I am.

Sometimes the circus comes to town.

I could be a dancing bear, reign devastation on these homes

of sod & tar paper, then lie down like a pet by the fire.

The chain around my neck, chafing.

Children would sink their paws into my oily brown fur. My Master

would brush me nightly, call me his dear one.

But I am irascible. I shall call on my Lord.

Where there is waste, growth will be forged.

This land shall be wild as the traveling troupe, these Great Plains

returned to the Garden our Mother Eve was in. Horehound, whorehouse—

all must be reckoned, arranged.

Some dance too close to strangers, let all the sugar go to their head.

Others skip town, complain; go insane.

THE MIND'S BOIL

whispers protruding like
  bones from the walls

     my glass
     appetite

       clinking keys proceed
        dose after
         dose

after
the first incident
  the doctor's hand
    (I tried to bite it off, like Johnny said)

  the nurse found other means
    of compulsion

her arms rope-strong

      My escape?
      I said accident
      (stepped too strong on necks)
       slipped hard across the land

Girls learn quick
  my body rosy-red
hair let loose
    Winter red flowers bloom on my palm
     hand wrapped in muslin
      (blocks the blood)
  the flesh loose, cold

     powdered potions
     fine as sand
     symptoms, in the dread hour of night:

                                         ice throat
                                         furred lips
            the mind's boil
strung high   follow orders

                        I escaped by smashing:

            smash sinful neighbor whores
                                                    smash barns

                    smash stores
"Fancy Mary, come to Town!"

JOHNNY'S DIARY

1

Johnny wants
to press feet
into ears,
catch whispers
to bury &
betray blood.

His favorite
farm is vacant
& aroused.
The chickens
scatter before
the full moon.
Knives planted
in the spring
harvest autumn
torture trees.

2

You know the scent
of shatter like I
know the mouth-feel
of icy thumbs,
peeling a bruised
nail at its seam,
overturning
a stone; the grimy
delights beneath
what we are meant
to see.

Climbing every oak
until stranded
like a child at the top.
Don't fear
the coming down.
Just fall softly.

3

Everything that is
given away easily—
or taken.

The skin of a father,
mother's hair,
bruises from a
brother or friend.

You would taste
so lovely in the
miniature room,
among the dolls
with china ears
& inconsolable
faces.

Bride & groom
tightly strung,
wounding promises
already. Be the tarnish
staining their fingers
so soon.

4

The metal scent
of change, that

lawless undertaker.
The courage of some
women to resist.
At nightfall, I lick
your eyelids free
& you are chary
with these pleasures.
Bless you, jilted bird,
meadow lark of wing-
busted toss.

Stained blood
in the garden,
lightning caught
in the trees.

I know the forecast:
tamed.

5

Whiskey breath female—
let the crows
take control. Remember
the dreams you made
of me—where do you want
me now? Let's rough
someone up, break
a window or two—
you're famous & full
of luck.

Steal a horse, take up
the mouth organ. Your
father sold you for an acorn.

You need my rough hand
at your back. The mirror

reflected wrong. So you
imagined I pinned you
in a haystack; you gave
me a son.

So much time on your
knees in the chapel.
This is no proper
marriage. Where has
the sting of my rope
gone to? What of hills
marred by the flashy
bulb of a photographer?
No God can remedy
your diagnosis:

All haunt, no house.

NEEDLE POINTING NORTH

The fire drove us out in zero-weather.
Amid the hubbub, I strayed.
My true asylum comes from my Master,
not this Most Unholy sacrilege.
Now my time is free for servitude
to Thee! (The eyes of Lunatics always
did shine brighter.) I shall make my trek—
crash through barriers Men build
before you. Make this quest my sacrament,
more blessed than Matrimony.

Precious powder is my Eucharist.
I take your Body inside me, finer
than crumbs of bread, Closer to me.
You make my heart race, Sir. My kerchief
is spotted with Evidence of your Redemption.

As a child, I longed to be a wild thing,
to slip off the back of the wagon & disappear
into the brush. I dreamt of the woods
where badgers would tend to me & I'd curl,
a little bald thing, between brothers & sisters.

The tenor of this land is ice; crystals form in my eyes
& blue my thumbs. I follow the hare through
the wood to his burrow. Nowise can I fit.

I climb trees high, fish seed out of pine cones
like a bird. Bears dance at midnight,
ferns rise up & scatter.
When my head grows hot, cool my temples, Johnny,
whisper fairy tales in German like grandmother
read in the dark. Crows menace the sheep & I dream,
900 miles from nowhere.

Once I lay down in a garden, secret & untamed.
Thorns tore at my bare feet. Armies flew tiny arrows
into my back as it touched the grass. Not all stories
can be contained among these flowers. I heard the sound
of weeping beyond the stone wall. A boy I hated threw
words like rocks. They smashed my glasses until
I saw clear. He pranced away, satisfied, a faun. I watered
the grass red & the geese on the path let me pass.

Master, the trees have tongues. No one believed me.

III

THE INABILITY TO HOLD PARTICLES TOGETHER

THE PUPIL

My hands gripped the edge of the couch.
Velvet, but fake velvet, & stained stiff
from the dog who spent all afternoon licking
himself & ejaculating onto the cushion. I
felt your hands on my breasts. Your fingers
were cold. My corduroy skirt made a sound
& caught, like it was stuck against
the velvet. You seemed to struggle, lifting it,
& I sat there staring at your paintings from
Africa on the wall behind me. I felt your
tongue inside my mouth & I wanted to bite
down, but I didn't. I couldn't breathe.

I answered the phone at my parents' house.
I knew it was your breathing. I could feel you
in my ear, soft & wet. Goose bumps rose up
on my arms & I crossed my legs. You started
telling me about the last time I saw you. You
reminded me of where your hands & fingers
& tongue & voice were. My mother looked
at the caller ID: "Oh, good, it's your
teacher!" & she left the room. I didn't know
how to disconnect. I didn't know how to—

There was no blood on my underwear afterward,
though I wanted to find it there. I wanted some
proof that you hurt me, but instead my grandmother
invited you in for lemonade, & I had to sit carefully
on the edge of her couch, because I thought I could
feel something coming back out from myself, pooling
in the spot where I was sitting & I didn't want anyone
to know because then I would have to tell them everything
& they would know what I am, just as you threatened.

Years later when I made love to my wife
I couldn't stop crying, & she left me
alone on the cold bathroom tile. *Tell me about your first time*,
she asked, & I couldn't forget the way you emptied me
onto your bathroom floor after our lessons. The coolness on my cheek,
& how swollen my lips grew. & afterward, how warm
you were against me. & when I became a teacher too,
you asked me if I would be like you.

No, I tell you, when we meet again
in my grandmother's garden, your ancient dress wilting,
still trying to pretend you are not fifty years my senior,
the lemonade glasses sweating on the table.
No, I don't remember anything.

THE SEASONS ARE EASY TO DISTINGUISH

I am pining for autumn. My friend is afraid.
                She fears if I name it, I will summon it.

She drapes her breasts in silk ribbons, binds them;
          I can see through her shirt.
                    When my wife began her affair,
she started wearing
          men's cologne, the same scent as my father.

I watched her leave as I stayed home. The latch clicked
          & I placed my nose on her pillow.

This continual fall & thrum;
                    the inability to hold particles together,
          to contain what we are trying to construct.

          My wilderness,
                    my wilds,
                        my wife:

                                    willing,
                                    willful.
She always called me coward.

& it's true:
                    yesterday, the river broke my thumb; the rapids
                      swallowed my scream.
I remembered the whitewater on our honeymoon, how I refused
                    to kayak alone.
                How she sought out disaffection, frenzy.
                      I napped naked in the hotel, dreaming
          of slipstream; my bare legs pointed toward the rocks,
the disequilibrium as I   fell

backward into the current.

Today there is a chill in the air, &

apples

on my tongue.

MORE EVIDENCE FOR THE DINOSAUR/BIRD LINK

Dear, I want to be bird-boned,
evolve into flight. Eyes like beads,
talons grip branches; bony bells & whistles;
feathered. Make me a nest of your body,
a safe place to roost.

I used to know so much about dinosaurs—
Iguanodon, Polacanthus, Pterosaur.
I used to climb trees, sleep in forests,
feast on flowers. Now I live in their land,

the lost continent of Utah. What is now desert,
once an ancient sea. On Sundays, we visit bones
& reckon diminutive. Allosaurus rivals T-Rex
as the supreme meat-eater of the Mesozoic.
We are fond of dominant predators.

I am thankful for my paleontologist bedfellow
who eats raw honeycomb from my hand,
takes my flesh between her teeth.
Metal rain drums the sky.

Sixty-eight million years asleep in the earth;
I am more ostrich than alligator.

Some trees shed their leaves;
                others lie dormant.

The estuary floods every summer
& come fall, when the bed is dry,
we sift through what has been left behind.

EXOSKELETON

Red birds beat their wings against the cage.
I think of you more often now that you're dead.
Your voice menaces my dreams—chases sleep
every night. Sometimes even my cat sees you.

You're drinking whiskey straight. You're dancing.
You told me a story: moving back to California
one summer, you ran out of room in your suitcases.
You had to wear all of your clothes—

they ballooned your body out,
like strangely soft exoskeletons. On the plane,
you stripped the sweaters off one by one,
until you bore only a white tank top, a tiny

eggshell. You were cold.
I live now on a canopy road
where branches of live oaks tangle together
over the street, eerie Spanish moss

dripping down like hair torn
out in a nightmare, casting spells
in whispers on the breeze. I drink
two nights a week with people who never

knew your name. I drink til I am sick
& you appear, smiling before me,
bobbing your head. I limit myself. If I drank
every day, I would join you.

The note you left—
you wanted to get to the other side,
but couldn't see a way. Now the wall seems high—
I tried to scale it twice

since hearing you'd traveled over.
Today I wear your dangly earrings
with bits of polished green shell skirting my neck.
I think of the night we shaved our heads—

feet of mousy locks liberated,
our pale napes, the remaining duck fluff
sticking up irregularly. You were a mirror
& we stood face to face, clasping hands.

THE SOUND OF WOODSMOKE

Tether. The shape of your lips,
an O to blow across the bottle.
I took your tail in my hands.
Shadow patterns, pine &
salt. The cedar smell of piñon.
I put the lime in my mouth.
I put the fakery.
Ribbon encircles your wrists.
Tightens.
I let my mouth rest there,
beside yours. I tasted breath
& blood.
Yesterday begat today.

INSOMNIA WITH SOLOMON

My mother calls. I should get a flu shot.
I should brush my hair & start saving
more money. I should tell who my soul
loveth & why I am called the fastest
among women. The neighbor's dog
continues to bark all night. I should use
CFL bulbs, stop eating red meat, take
the train to work more often. I should
call the keeper of my vineyards & ask,
red or white with edamame? I should
adorn my neck with chains of gold, let
my lover lie all night betwixt my breasts.
But she snores! I should vacuum, take
the trash to the chute, get my car washed,
have my eggs harvested, find a sperm
donor, because the sun hath looked upon
me & mine own vineyard I haven't kept.
The book I left at the office, was it under
a stack of papers, or had it fallen to the floor?
Why did I forget the book I forgot? Is it
worth fighting football traffic on Saturday
to read the venerated essay on why I should
never end a line in a poem on the word the?
I should not stir up nor awake my love
til she please. Lord knows she works hard
for the money while I pet the cat & google
sperm donors. The tender grape gives a good
smell. But the little foxes spoil the vines.
I should pay more attention to fertility,
the importance of female orgasm in conception,
how analogous heterosexual positions are
to lesbian ones. By night on my bed, I sought
sleep. I sought him, but I found him not.

If every man hath his sword upon his thigh,
where should a lesbian keep her sword?
We keep ours in the bedside table drawer.
I should unload the dishwasher tomorrow,
buy birdseed & bread. I should stop gazing
at houses I cannot afford, houses with fountains
of gardens & a well of living waters. I wish
my lover would blow upon my garden more.
This blanket is too light for the growing chill;
I should find the down quilt in the basement.
I should wash these sheets tomorrow, fold last
week's laundry. I should really get some sleep.
I should spend more time calling my mother.

SWEET ALBATROSS

Dear wingspan,
dear vagrant,
dear soar & slope.

I can feel you mourning me
from this far away.

I am a cephalopod; your beak
seeks me.

O diver, I will use your wingbones
to tattoo ceremony onto my skin.

But my crossbow shoots like the stars;
I fear no curse or necklace made from prey.

Plastic flotsam catches
in your gizzard, & I hear you caw.

I can feel your flightpath,
your feathertrade.

You are my bad luck charm,
planting your webs on my deck,
menacing me.

Sweet albatross, you miss me.
For the life of the pair,
you are said to remain constant.

I am an island in the middle of the sea;
you are flying out of range.

TENDER :: THROB

She does me from behind,
her free hand tangled
in my hair, so that my face
points to the ceiling. Using
a knee she spreads my legs
farther apart & I instinctively
buck back into her harder.

Common :
cramp :
surge.

My arms give out & I rest
my face against the mattress
as she hugs the swell of my ass,
lowers her lips & leaves a bruise.
I am a vice grip around her wrist.

Tattoo :
tongue :
come.

She slides her hand slowly
out of me, a rush of fluid & blood
as next door, the neighbor
eavesdrops on our arias.

Torn :
tendril :
empty.

We pause to see if the bleeding
will stop, me on my back now,
             one knee resting atop her shoulder,
like we are stretching. One finger
             excavates. I feel cavernous.

                                   Gone :
                                          fist :
                  flight.

        The bleeding slows.
Her hands grip my hips, pull me
             onto her strap-on.
I bite my lip, guide her hand
             to my breast as the other gently
cradles my neck.

INSTRUCTIONS FOR UNEXPECTED HOUSEGUESTS

The Lady moon brings visitors
unforeseen. The Pink moon—
we light the grapefruit candle.

Drive the five & a half hours
from Winnemucca, midway
between here & San Francisco.
Water at the Buckaroo Hall of Fame.

Tie a red rope around your waist.
Grow accustomed   (costumed)
to the dust that settles on everything.
The wind brings it from the West.

Red Raspberry Leaf tea. Nettles.
Dandelion root. Blue & Black
cohosh. In a tincture or a tea.
Unravel winter's sweater for
tomorrow's blanket. Purl.

Guests arrive at dusk to find work,
take care of business,
& have a bit of pleasure.

The ring around the moon means trouble.

An infusion of parsley. Vitamin C.
Basil, honey, nutmeg. Mandrake root.
Stand with your back to the wind.
Draw three circles, clockwise, around the plant with a knife.
Douse it with Mary Water. Turn West to uproot.

FRIPPERY & DEMISE

Always imaginative, sometimes
        imaginary, we tied thin red ribbons
                around our necks in honor of you :
the necklace of blood that bloomed
        at the Revolution. Pristine & filthy
                you wore the ocean in your hair.
From youth we learn to manipulate
        & adorn the female form. Ball gowns,
                afternoon dresses, robes & petticoats
in a score of delicate shades, the silks
        embroidered with floral designs &
                silk ribbon appliqué, the borders trimmed
with serpentine garlands of silver & gold
        lace, fields of artificial flowers, feathers,
                tassels & silk ribbon bows, rosettes
& ruffles, *passementerie* & beading & metallic fringe.
        Even for a queen, your trousseau was a spectacular one.
Covered in sapphires on your coronation,
        the weight of hair & dress held you down.
                Your face seemed the midpoint between
top of the hair & hem of the gown & your neck showed
        no sign of bowing under the strain.
                For death you dressed in white: plum-black
shoes, a fresh white underskirt & the immaculate chemise.
        Around your neck the prettiest muslin fichus,
                the ruffled linen bonnet as colorless as your hair.
A figure of pure, radiant white. The color of a ghost too beautiful.

LETTER TO A.

The children I teach have learned your name. It was what came to mind when they asked for a word with X in the center. They are studying how to form letters, what shape to make with their pencil connecting one thing to the next.

At night, I listen to dogs barking on distant farms. My cat walks up & down my body & settles on my chest. Sometimes I wake up startled, imagining it is your hand pinning me down. In my dreams, your thin arms are housed in silk chiffon, a fabric that is easily torn.

M. tells me you've found a job. At the cat hospital, you help the nurses boil skulls, reconstructing those fragile skeletons for display.

No lapsing, love. Put my stories out like a cigarette. Extend our summer. Think on the codes we memorized but never used, raw corn gobbled from the cob, the mirror reflecting wrong.

Tell your mother there are some curses that cannot be reversed.

The sun has reached the north wall, & I must close. I'll chastise the students for you, the very bad little girls who braid their hair together. I'll pull them asunder.

ANGER ENDURES

Last year you weren't dead.
Last year we drank beer fermented in raspberries
& laughed til it came out our noses.

We held hands, wore blue,
closed our eyes & spun around until the ground
rose up to greet us.

Your mother sends me a prayer card.
On one side is an angel.
On one side is your picture & a date.

Your name was magic,
juju your mother concocted to protect you,
combining letters from both grandmas' names.

You swathed yourself in orange, made
mammoth salads for health & assembled
bouquets for beauty. Everything a spell.

I didn't go to your funeral.
In bed, alone, my hands pressed my eyes
until no tears dared to drop.

You're not a star in the sky.
You're not watching or listening
or sending messages through the television.

You're dead this year
& no one knows how.
I didn't go to your funeral

because I don't forgive you

& that fear persists;
the ash clings to my fingernails.

You haven't met my kitten
or swum in my pool.
You didn't vote.

AVIAN NIGHTMARE

A sky that blue is not American.
This dream must be set

on the Mediterranean shores.
& that parakeet perched

on a park bench might be you.
Are you fleeing the mistral

or me, both with our dry coldness?
If I call you by a name known only

in dreams, if I speak the word *darling*, watch—
you swiftly fly to my finger,

weary of the weather.
Your breast is greener than I'd

expected, black dots like a necklace
before your shock of yellow head.

I've never had a bird to sing to me,
forgive me if I don't know the routine.

Do you take requests?
Whistle for me & blink distantly.

What does it mean that my mind has given you wings?

I NEVER WEAR DRESSES, BUT I'LL DO IT FOR YOU

J. said he'd pay us a quarter each if we'd kiss & let him watch.
He wanted us on his lap together.

We wore red dresses.
It's important in dreams for the women to match.

We took the money & blindfolded him,
& he chased us on his knees.

We licked gin off his ice cubes,
straws sticking the backs of our throats.

Now our nails have grown too long to love each other,
the parties too tired to be interested in our show.

You fed me potpourri like your mother kept in bowls
around the house, hosed me down in the backyard
& rubbed sugar into my hair.

You strapped me to the rock we pretended was a casket
when we were children. The boys tied us down,
made us close our eyes & pay the toll to the underworld.

We untied the knots more easily without an audience.

THE MARGIN OF THE LAKE

On the shores   a heavy sound

I wore a dress of whisper   to touch it feels smooth   surprise

my face now flame colored

I know not why   I will not quarrel with myself

dull & melancholy

the moonshine herrings in the water

disturbed me even more than when I have been happier

& the storm that followed

we closed our eyes & listened to the sirens

my head bad & I lay long

the last glimpse of twilight it calls the heart home to quietness

ONE DAY I LAID DOWN THE BRUISE OF YOU

In those five-inch stilettos,
she thought you were fierce.
You wanted to patent-leather wound.

But I was watching the entire time.

Rubber suit, leather crotch, paper cut,
lucky dragon, loose buttons, dirty feet.

If this is the nadir, my wrist is already broken;
hit me with everything—
slanted wigs, rotten fruit, shattered glass.

But no more on my knees at the keyhole.
No smeared-lip vendetta. Your nomad cunt
keeps coming back, but the locks have frozen,
the whip gone missing.

Once I sat alone in a velvet theater.
I imagined you inside me.
That was enough.

Tiny fist curled, like a bird:
wings beating in the nest.

A pocketful of feathers.

Most accidents happen close to home.

MENACE

I traveled unaccompanied around the world
& landed here, bereft.
This is not the story I told
you the first night.

Between pages of books I press leaves
& letters. My bones shift.
I have no weapon, no lance
against danger, just memory.

When you come around, the lock
breaks. The rain stains the windows,
the vegetable bin is full of lack.
I try to lie very still.

The cold enters my room; the chain
on the door holds fast. I tighten
my belt, press my hand to my cheek,
where your tongue tasted iron.

BENEDICTION

We learn to say memory phonetically,
the placement of tongue on teeth.

I have forgotten the compression of snow,
how often *were* & *wish* appear in my speech.

This year: more verbs, more letters, less illness.
Travel: landscapes of red rock rising from the road,
salt water. Clean air. No humidity.

My only pains, champagnes.
My only monsters the ones I invited in.

Hands clutching my back,
men's hats & handkerchiefs.
Braids & blondes.

I used to wear a black sweater every day.
This year I will wear a green one.

CONSOLATION

Where is winter kept?

Lace :: Delicate tatting.

I dream often:

motorcycles, ovaries, slickrock, stomach amputation.

The garment was not merely adornment.

Well-tended, leaves still scatter.

Have I not worn gold around my neck?

Fearing the cold, remember the luxurious birds.

Tailfeathers braided together.

How willingly you forget the farmland.

Inside, by the hearth you burned my maiden name.

A ring :: a strand of ice.

Understanding the quick dark.

In the storm, a swerve.

You promised to hold your breath until it froze.

Simple, my own style of dress, until I discovered delicacy.

Whose garment fell to the floor?

Who opened the gate & released such a season?

NOTES

The italicized lines in "Tornado Alley" come from an America Forever anti-gay political action committee pamphlet.

"Grammar for Everyone" was inspired by the French grammar book *La Becherelle: La grammaire pour tous*. Throughout the exercises in the book, the same characters reappear, so that as one builds language skills, a narrative is formed.

"Remarks on Color" is after Wittgenstein.

"Your Body Will Haunt Mine" takes its title from Adrienne Rich's "Twenty-one Love Poems."

In "Unlike Your Sister," the line "You need something new & I am new" comes from a Josh Bell poem, "Epithalamium, Ex Post Facto."

Mary Sweeney was a real woman, a "window-smasher" who traveled the upper Midwest during the late nineteenth century. Little is known about her, but she was institutionalized several times and escaped. I first learned of her in the book *Wisconsin Death Trip* by Michael Lesy.

"Prayer" is a reworking of Psalm 139 in the King James Bible.

In "Johnny's Diary" the lines "Let me instill the pain surgeons assuage" and "All haunt, no house," are paraphrases of Emily Dickinson. I first heard the latter from Mark Wunderlich.

In "Needle Pointing North," the line "900 miles from nowhere" is quoted from an actual homesteader's letter, as found in Steven Kinsella's book of the same title.

"Frippery & Demise" is about Marie Antoinette. Details of her wardrobe were taken from the book *Queen of Fashion: What Marie Antoinette Wore to the Revolution* by Caroline Weber.

"The margin of the lake" is an erasure of lines from Dorothy Wordsworth's *Grasmere & Alfoxden Journals*.

ACKNOWLEDGMENTS

Thank you to the editors of the following journals in which some of these poems first appeared:

The Account: A Journal of Poetry, Prose & Thought	I gave you my—— The sound of woodsmoke
Animal	More Evidence for the Dinosaur/Bird Link
burnt district	Consolation
Dangerous Sweetness	Tornado Alley
Dressing Room Poetry Journal	Mysterious Acts by My People
La Fovea	Avian Nightmare Late Russian
Jenny Magazine	Frippery & Demise
The Journal	Anatomy
Keep Going	Exoskeleton
Ink Node	The seasons are easy to distinguish
Main Street Rag	Anger Endures
Melusine	Twins
PANK Magazine	Bad Wife Spankings Insomnia with Solomon July Love Poem in Three Parts
Poemmemoirstory	One day I laid down the bruise of you
Sugar House Review	Benediction
Western Humanities Review	Solitary Vice Needle Pointing North
Word Riot	Grammar for Everyone I Never Wear Dresses, But I'd Do It For You

GRATITUDE

I am grateful to my communities of friends and teachers at Bennington College, Florida State University, and the University of Utah for their generosity and support. Special thanks to Chandler Klang Smith, Rebecca Godwin, Mark Wunderlich, Pete Kunze, Rebecca Lehmann, C.A. Schaefer, Erin Rogers, Meg Day, Tasha Matsumoto, Catie Crabtree, Barbara Duffey, Stephen S. Mills, Katharine Coles, Paisley Rekdal, Anne Jamison, and Karen Brennan. To my NOLOSE community: thank you for sustaining me. Thanks to the Lambda Literary Foundation whose generous scholarship to the Emerging LGBT Writers' Retreat enabled me to write many of these poems, and to my Lambda family for warmly welcoming them and me.

For those who gave me feedback on some of these poems, all my gratitude: Peter Gizzi, D. Gilson, Myung Mi Kim, Ellen Bass, Jenny Boully, Matthew Zapruder, Brigit Pegeen Kelly, and Wayne Koestenbaum.

I am enormously grateful to Scott Sweeney of Grey Book Press, the editors at Gertrude Press, and Kristen Stone at Unthinkable Creatures Chapbook Press for first collecting some of these poems in the chapbooks *Scent of Shatter* (2010), *Bad Wife Spankings* (2011) and *nostrums: a handbook of the unborn* (2013).

Thank you to Bryan Borland, Seth Pennington, and everyone who contributes to the success of Sibling Rivalry Press; thank you for choosing this book and bringing it into the world. I'm proud to be part of the family.

Finally, all my love and thanks to my family for their unconditional love and support.

ABOUT THE POET

Valerie Wetlaufer is a birth doula, teacher, editor, and poet. She holds a BA in French and an MA in Teaching from Bennington College, an MFA in Poetry from Florida State University, and a PhD in Literature & Creative Writing from the University of Utah, where she was a Vice Presidential Fellow. Born and raised in Iowa, Valerie has since lived in Vermont, Paris, Minnesota, Arizona, Florida, and Utah. She has been nominated for several Pushcart Prizes. In 2010, she was a Fellow at the Lambda Literary Foundation's Emerging Writers Retreat. Valerie is the author of three chapbooks, *Scent of Shatter* (Grey Book Press 2010), *Bad Wife Spankings* (Gertrude Press 2011), and *Nostrums* (Unthinkable Creatures Press 2013), and the editor of *Adrienne: a Poetry Journal of Queer Women*. She lives in Cedar Rapids, Iowa.

ABOUT THE COVER ARTIST

Zeke Tucker is a Christian graphic designer and photographer from Chattanooga, Tennessee, originally from Maryville, Tennessee. A 23-year-old newlywed, he has five siblings, three of whom are adopted. He loves chaos, organization, and instant film. He has a large collection of Polaroid cameras. Visit him online at www.society6.com/zeketucker.

ABOUT THE PRESS

Founded in 2010, Sibling Rivalry Press is an independent publishing house based in Alexander, Arkansas. Our mission is to publish work that disturbs and enraptures. For more information, visit www.siblingrivalrypress.com.

CPSIA information can be obtained
at www.ICGtesting.com
Printed in the USA
FFOW02n0533211114
8868FF

9 781937 420666